California DMV Driver's Handbook

Practice for the California Permit Test with 350+ Driving Questions and Answers

By: Discover Prep

Foreword

In order to obtain your learner's permit, you must score at least an 85% on your permit test.

This book will prepare you with the knowledge you will need to earn a passing grade on your learner's permit exam.

The Department of Motor Vehicles in your state issues official driving manuals that contain valuable resources that you must be familiar with and know about. If that information overrides anything in this manual, be sure to memorize it and use it.

To achieve success with this book, use this as a fundamental tool to help guide and better prepare you for the questions you will need to answer in order to pass your exam.

The driving exam features a variety of questions that will gauge your quick-thinking skills and require you to use common sense. The questions featured in this book will help you to understand what to expect come test time and will help better your chances of earning your learner's permit.

How to Use This Book

This book is best used by starting at the beginning, working through to the end, and taking time to think through each scenario. Applying your comprehension skills to best assess each question in detail will allow you to gain a better understanding and prepare you for your learner's permit exam. Imagining each scenario will help you to recall that image on the test itself.

You can choose to practice with an adult or a partner or read the questions aloud to yourself to retain them more easily. Practice is key, and this book is closely modeled after the chapters from the DMV manual.

Another good study technique is to use an index card to cover the answer choices, then read the scenario and question. Stop and think to yourself what the answer should be, then look for it in the choices. Most of the time you can identify it because you studied the correct information, and you can move on. If not immediately identified, go back to the question (not the whole scenario) being asked and eliminate answers until you get one that seems correct. Practicing like this will help you during the test because you won't get distracted by all of the choices and you'll be able to move quickly through any timed test.

By studying this book, you will be prepared, ready, and more likely to have better success when it comes to passing your exam. On average, nearly 50% of teenagers fail the exam on their first attempt. Allow this book to be the guide you need to earn a passing grade the first time.

Disclaimer: Due to frequently changing laws, please refer to your official local DMV manual for the most up-to-date answers and explanations.

ROAD SIGNS

Questions & Answers

1. When you see this sign, you are entering a section of road that contains:

    A. An emergency vehicle.
    B. A school zone.
  ✗ C. A flagger.
    D. A construction crew.

Correct Answer is C. A flagger. These signs let you know that a flagger, visible by their orange vests and SLOW/STOP signs, may direct you on the road ahead.

2. What do you do when you see this sign?

    A. Turn twice, first left and then right.
    B. Speed up to get over a hill.
  ✗ C. Watch out for a sharp turn.
    D. Slow down up ahead.

Correct Answer is D. Slow down up ahead. This sign means that a slippery road could cause an accident, so drivers need to check their speed on the road coming up.

3. A sign with this shape can only mean that this road:

    A. Is a two-way road.
    B. Is a no-zone.
    C. Is a road with merging traffic.
    D. Is a no-passing zone.

Correct Answer is D. Is a no-passing zone. Signs with this shape
mean that you cannot pass drivers going in your direction.
These signs are always on the left side of the road.

4. What does the line and arrow on this sign indicate?

    ✗A. A winding road
    B. A double curve
    C. A right turn
    D. A slow curve to the right

Correct Answer is A. A winding road. This sign means that the
road ahead will wind and that you should slow down, stay to the
right, and refrain from passing.

5. This sign will direct you to a:

A. Highway
B. Hospital
C. Hotel
D. Hangar

Correct Answer is B. Hospital. These signs inform drivers that they are close to a medical facility.

6. This sign with a silhouette of two people means that you should:

A. Keep an eye out for shoppers in busy districts.
B. Slow down for a pedestrian crosswalk.
C. Slow down as you pass through a school zone.
D. Both B and C

Correct Answer is D. Both B and C. This sign indicates a pedestrian crosswalk. When in a school zone, schoolchildren may be crossing the street and you need to proceed with caution. Pay attention to the lowered speed limits.

7. When you see a sign with a bicycle on it, you should know that:

    A. Bicyclists aren't allowed to ride here.
    B. The road ahead crosses with a bikeway.
  ✗C. This road has a path for bicyclists and drivers should be careful.
    D. Bicyclists cannot pass in the area up ahead.

Correct Answer is B. The road ahead crosses with a bikeway. This sign is also called a bicycle crossing and tells you to be cautious of cyclists on the road ahead.

8. This sign means that you CANNOT make a left turn here.

    A. True
    B. False

Correct Answer is A. True.

9. What is up ahead when you see this sign?

    A. A narrow bridge
    B. Train tracks
    C. A steep hill
    D. A one-way road

Correct Answer is A. A narrow bridge. This sign warns you that a bridge or overpass is located ahead, and it has minimal clearance. Keep to your lane and drive with caution.

10. This sign means that:

    A. A road under repair is just ahead.
    B. You're about to cross a highway junction.
    C. A railroad crossing is coming up.
    D. Your road is closed, and you need to find a turn-off.

Correct Answer is C. A railroad crossing is coming up. This sign tells you to slow down and look out for the warning signals that tell you when to stop at the tracks. Keep on the lookout for the same RXR on the ground near the tracks, as it is on this sign.

11. This sign indicates a:

A. Crossroads
B. Hospital
C. Railroad crossing
D. Crosswalk

12. This sign means that:

A. Trucks should not use this road.
B. Drivers should watch for trucks on the road ahead.
C. The road slopes downhill ahead.
D. Heavy trucks need to slow down.

13. This sign means:

    A. You cannot enter.
    B. You cannot park.
    C. You cannot turn.
    D. You cannot stop.

Correct Answer is A. You cannot enter. This is a No Entry road sign and indicates a road that unauthorized vehicles cannot use.

14. This sign indicates a railroad crossing up ahead.

    A. True
    B. False

Correct Answer is B. False. This sign indicates a pharmacy up ahead.

15. This sign means that for the road up ahead:

    A. The speed limit is 50 mph and you can't drop below 30 in ideal conditions.

    B. The speed limit is 50 mph in normal conditions, but you should slow down to 30 when it's raining.

    C. The speed limit is 50 mph when at least 30 cars are driving on it.

    D. The speed limit is 50 mph, with a minimum fine of $30 for speeding.

Correct Answer is A. The speed limit on this road is 50 mph and you can't drop below 30 in ideal conditions.

16. This sign means that up ahead:

    A. Traffic merges from the right.

    B. Traffic merges from the left.

    C. Traffic splits into two lanes.

    D. Traffic will enter an intersection.

Correct Answer is A. Traffic merges from the right. This sign tells drivers that mergers will be joining from the right with traffic on the road ahead.

17. What should you do when you see this sign?

    A. Watch for a hidden road.
    B. Watch for slippery turns.
    C. Watch for a low road shoulder.
    D. Watch for gravel or other obstructions.

Correct Answer is C. Watch for a low road shoulder. This sign indicates that the shoulder drops beneath the surface of the road.

18. This road sign indicates a forest zone ahead.
    A. True
    B. False

Correct Answer is B. False. This sign indicates that a rest area is coming up on the right.

19. What should you do when you come to a yield sign?

    A. Move ahead while other cars yield to you.
    B. Slow down to yield to cars crossing your path.
    C. Stop your car to yield to oncoming traffic.
    D. Prepare to yield as you cross a no-passing zone.

Correct Answer is B. Slow down to yield to cars crossing your path. Yield signs mean that you should give other cars the right of way and move forward slowly. Do not stop unless the way is not clear.

20. What does this sign mean?

    A. You cannot make a U-turn.
    B. You cannot go straight.
    C. You can only turn in the arrow's direction.
    D. You cannot turn at all.

Correct Answer is A. You cannot make a U-turn. This sign indicates that it's not safe to U-turn to the opposite direction from that lane.

21. What does this sign indicate?

A. You should refrain from turning left at this intersection.
B. You should only turn left at this intersection.
C. You must turn left in the left lane but can turn left or go straight in the right lane.
D. You must turn left in the left lane but can either go straight or turn left at the next intersection in the right lane.

Correct Answer is C. You must turn left in the left lane but can turn left or go straight in the right lane.

22. The center lane sign means that:

A. Cars in the center lane may turn left or pass while driving from either direction.
B. Cars in the center lane must turn left when driving in either direction and cannot pass.
C. Cars in the center lane cannot turn right or left when driving in either direction.
D. Cars in the left lane must turn left.

Correct Answer is B. Cars in the center lane must turn left when driving in either direction and cannot pass. This sign indicates the center lane is reserved for left turns in which you cannot pass other cars.

23. What does a sign with a "T" on it mean?

    A. Tourist information center ahead.
    B. Public telephone ahead.
    C. 4-way intersection ahead.
    D. The roadway ends ahead, and you must turn left or right.

Correct Answer is D. The roadway ends ahead, and you must turn left or right.

24. What does this sign mean you should do?

    A. Stay to the left of an obstacle.
    B. Stay to the right of an obstacle.
    C. Keep right because the left lane is ending.
    D. Stop for workers before continuing to the right.

Correct Answer is B. Stay to the right of an obstacle. This sign means that an obstruction is coming up, and you need to stay to the right of it.

25. What is coming up ahead when you see this sign?

    A. Road construction flagger
    B. Pedestrian crossing
    C. Snow removal worker
    D. Road workers near the road

Correct Answer is D. Road workers near the road. This sign indicates road workers working near the roadway. Slow down and pay attention to where they are.

KNOWLEDGE
Questions & Answers

1. When two lanes travel in the same direction and you are not allowed to pass, the road is lined with:

    A. A single yellow line.
    B. A yellow line and a white line.
    C. A double yellow line.
    D. A double white line.

Correct Answer is D. A double white line. Solid white lines indicate two lanes traveling in one direction. You should not try to pass if the lines are solid.

2. When the weather and driving conditions are normal, you should maintain a following distance between your car and the car in front of you equal to:

    A. 1 second
    B. 2 seconds
    C. 4 seconds
    D. 6 seconds

Correct Answer is C. 4 seconds. Tailgating, or following too closely, raises your risk for rear-end collisions. Maintaining 4 seconds of driving distance in normal conditions is a good rule of thumb.

3. You are on a drawbridge and you see a red signal. What do you do?

    A. Stop at the line.
    B. Slow down and proceed with caution.
    C. Yield to oncoming traffic.
    D. Make a U-turn to avoid the obstruction.

Correct Answer is A. Stop at the line. The light means that the bridge is in operation. You must stop at the line until the road opens again.

4. If you see the car behind you is trying to pass, what should you do?

    A. Slow down a bit. Remain in your lane.
    B. Pull to the right. Stop so the car can pass.
    C. Blow your horn. Let the car pass.
    D. Keep your speed the same. Let traffic continue to smoothly flow.

Correct Answer is A. Slow down a bit. Remain in your lane. Let the car pass without making drastic changes. Speed back up to your normal speed when the car has passed.

5. When parallel parking, make sure that:

    A. Your wheels touch the curb.
    B. Your wheels are within 18 inches of the curb.
    C. Your wheels are within 28 inches of the curb.
    D. Your wheels are at least 3 feet from the curb.

Correct Answer is B. Your wheels are within 18 inches of the curb. This is close enough to keep the roads clear.

6. If you fail to submit the results of a blood alcohol test your license will be suspended, even on your first offense. How long will the suspension last?

    A. 3 months
    B. 6 months
    C. 12 months
    D. 24 months

Correct Answer is C. 12 months. This can vary depending on your state, but 12 months is the most common length of suspension. Check with your state's DMV if you want to know more.

7. You approach an intersection at the same time, approximately, as another car. Who can move into the intersection first?

    A. The driver on the left.
    B. The driver on the right.
    C. The driver who turns on their signal first.
    D. The drivers can move at the same time.

Correct Answer is B. The driver on the right. In this situation, drivers must yield to the right, so that driver can move first.

8. While waiting at a railroad crossing without a crossbuck, the train has passed. What should you do?

    A. Drive quickly across the tracks before another train comes.
    B. Honk your horn and cross the tracks.
    C. Wait for the light to turn green so you can go safely.
    D. Look for additional trains and drive cautiously.

Correct Answer is D. Look for additional trains, and drive cautiously. At railroad crossings, you won't get lights telling you to stop and go. If the tracks are clear, check for oncoming trains, and proceed.

9. What is a speed limit?

    A. The minimum legal speed in any weather.
    B. The minimum legal speed in normal weather.
    C. The maximum legal speed in any weather.
    D. The maximum legal speed in normal weather.

Correct Answer is D. The maximum legal speed in normal weather.

10. What should you do if you miss your exit on the interstate?

    A. Reverse to your exit.
    B. Make a U-turn to your exit.
    C. Keep driving to the next exit.
    D. Stop your car.

Correct Answer is C. Keep driving to the next exit. If you miss an exit on the interstate, you can't turn around or reverse. Keep moving forward.

11. A flashing yellow arrow means that you should:

    A. Stop right away.
    B. Turn where the arrow is pointing after yielding to
        oncoming traffic.
    C. Turn where the arrow is pointing right away.
    D. Prepare to stop as the light turns red.

Correct Answer is B. Turn where the arrow is pointing after
yielding to oncoming traffic. Yield to the traffic that has no
signal to stop. Turn with caution.

12. The most important safety tip for drivers is:

    A. Don't drive as much.
    B. Always keep to the right where traffic is slower.
    C. Limit when you drive to less busy hours.
    D. Wear a seatbelt at all times.

Correct Answer is D. Wear a seatbelt at all times. This prevents
injuries more often than any other driving tips.

13. When are you allowed to block an intersection?

    A. When traffic is backed up.
    B. When you are entering a green light.
    C. When your car breaks down.
    D. You are never allowed to block an intersection.

Correct Answer is D. You are never allowed to block an intersection. Avoid going through a green or yellow light if traffic is backing up into the intersection so you don't block it.

14. A shared center lane allows drivers from both directions to:

    A. Make left turns.
    B. Make right turns.
    C. Slow down.
    D. Stop and back up.

Correct Answer is A. Make left turns. A shared center lane or two-way left-turn lane allows cars from both directions to turn left.

15. When entering a main road from a side road like a driveway or alley, what should you do?

    A. Refrain from turning right.
    B. Speed up and join the ongoing traffic.
    C. Slow down and join the ongoing traffic.
    D. Yield to cars and join the ongoing traffic at normal speed.

Correct Answer is D. Yield to cars, and join the ongoing traffic at normal speed. Make sure to yield to oncoming traffic.

16. Never cross railroad tracks when:

    A. The train traffic is busy that day.
    B. The lane is backed up on the other side.
    C. You have small children in the car.
    D. You hear a train in the distance.

Correct Answer is B. The lane is backed up on the other side. If the tracks are clear, you can cross so long as the lane isn't backed up.

17. For drivers 21 years old or younger, you can be convicted of driving under the influence with a blood alcohol level of:

    A. At least .02%
    B. At least .05%
    C. At least .08%
    D. At least .1%

Correct answer is A. At least .02%. Even this blood alcohol level counts as a DUI for drivers under the age of 21.

18. A broken yellow line on the road means that:

    A. Both lanes are moving in the opposite direction.
    B. Both lanes are moving in the same direction.
    C. Neither lane can pass other cars.
    D. Both lanes can drive in either direction.

Correct answer is A. Both lanes are moving in the opposite direction. A broken yellow line can be crossed if the road is clear.

19. In roundabouts, cars drive:

A. Clockwise.
B. Counterclockwise.
C. The direction indicated by the roundabout sign.
D. Whichever direction the driver wants.

Correct Answer is B. Counterclockwise. Yield to traffic before entering the roundabout. Traffic always moves counterclockwise.

20. If you need to use your hand to signal a right turn, your arm should be:

A. Extended backward.
B. Extended downward.
C. Extended upward.
D. Extended outward.

Correct Answer is C. Extended upward at a 90-degree angle.

21. Always turn on your _____ when driving in fog.

    A. Hazard signal
    B. Parking light
    C. High-beam headlights
    D. Low-beam headlights

Correct Answer is D. Low-beam headlights.

22. When trying to pass a car moving slower than you on a two-lane road, you should always:

    A. Use the shoulder.
    B. Use the oncoming lane.
    C. Flash your lights.
    D. Honk your horn.

Correct Answer is B. Use the oncoming lane. If you see that it's clear, you can pass the slower-moving car by using the oncoming lane. Leave your lights and horn alone.

23. You are never allowed to pass the car in front of you when:

A. The car is parallel parking.
B. The car is turning left.
C. The car is stopped at a crosswalk.
D. The car is on a one-way street with two lanes.

Correct Answer is C. The car is stopped at a crosswalk. If they're stopped, they could be waiting for a pedestrian to cross. It is never legal to pass them at this time.

24. What does "Dip" mean when you see it on a road sign?

A. There's a narrow bridge coming up.
B. There's a low area in the road coming up.
C. There's a high area in the road coming up.
D. The road is going to end soon.

Correct Answer is B. There's a low area in the road coming up. Depressions can fill with water and make driving more difficult.

25. While on the road, be sure to leave space between you and the other cars:

    A. In front
    B. Behind you
    C. On the left and right
    D. All the above

Correct Answer is D. All the above. Always make sure to leave space on all sides.

26. What is a restricted lane?

    A. A lane that pedestrians may be using.
    B. A lane with toll booths.
    C. A lane reserved for left or right turns.
    D. A lane reserved for certain vehicles.

Correct Answer is D. A lane reserved for certain vehicles. Don't turn into a restricted lane unless you are driving the vehicle type it is intended for.

27. How long should you use your turn signal for before getting to your turn?

    A. When you start the turn
    B. When you're 50 feet from the turn
    C. When you're 100 feet from the turn
    D. When you're in eyesight of the turn

Correct Answer is C. When you're 100 feet from the turn.

28. While driving on a highway, you want to turn right onto a two-lane road. Which lane do you use?

    A. The lane nearest to the curb
    B. The lane nearest to the center lane
    C. The lane with the least traffic
    D. Either A or B

Correct Answer is A. The lane nearest to the curb.

29. What distractions should you avoid in the car?

    A. Eating

    B. Listening to the radio

    C. Using your phone

    D. All the above

Correct Answer is D. All the above. Avoid as many distractions as possible while on the road.

30. When you sell your car, you must notify your state's DMV within:

    A. Five days.

    B. Ten days.

    C. One month.

    D. One year.

Correct Answer is A. Five days.

31. When are roads the most slippery due to rain?

    A. After it has rained for at least an hour.
    B. The day after heavy rain.
    C. As soon as it's no longer raining.
    D. For 10 minutes after the rain starts.

Correct Answer is D. For 10 minutes after the rain starts. This is when the roads are most slippery. The water mixes with debris on the road, like dust and oil slicks, and reduces traction between your wheels and the road, causing you to slip.

32. You can park in a disabled space with a tag, even if the disabled person is not in the car.

    A. True
    B. False

Correct Answer is B. False. Only the tagholder can legally park in the disabled space. They don't have to be driving, however—they can be a passenger as well.

33. What is the safest speed to drive?

    A. Slower is always safer.
    B. The speed limit is always safe.
    C. The safest speed changes based on the driving conditions.
    D. The same speed as the surrounding traffic.

Correct Answer is C. The safest speed changes based on the driving conditions.

34. Large trucks must turn a little differently on a two-lane road. When you see a big truck turning right, expect to see:

    A. The truck switching lanes.
    B. The truck holding to the shoulder they're turning toward.
    C. The truck using parts of both lanes to complete the turn.
    D. The truck stopping to let traffic pass them before turning.

Correct Answer is C. The truck using parts of both lanes to complete the turn. Big trucks often need to use parts of the left lane to make a right turn.

35. On slippery roads, make sure you:

    A. Follow at a greater distance.
    B. Stay closer to the cars in front of you.
    C. Find an alternate road to use.
    D. Drive as you would in any conditions.

Correct Answer is A. Follow at a greater distance. On slippery roads, cars will take longer to stop. Increase your following distance to stay safe.

36. If you're stopped and want to rejoin ongoing traffic, make sure you:

    A. Signal and wait for at least two cars to pass.
    B. Signal and wait for enough space to get up to the speed of the traffic.
    C. Make sure you drive slower than ongoing traffic for 100 feet.
    D. Make sure you speed up fast enough to overtake the traffic.

Correct Answer is B. Signal and wait for enough space to get up to the speed of the traffic.

37. Driving at night is:

A. Less dangerous than driving during the day.
B. More dangerous than driving during the day.
C. Just as dangerous as driving during the day.
D. All of the above.

Correct Answers is B. More dangerous than driving during the day. Adjust your speed according to the visibility.

38. It is legal to pass a car on the right if it is:

A. About to turn left.
B. About to turn right.
C. Turning to the left.
D. Turning to the right.

Correct Answer is A. About to turn left. If a car is waiting to turn left, you can pass it on the right, but not if it is currently turning.

39. Alcohol affects your driving skills in what way?

A. It impairs your reaction time, but not your decision-making.
B. It impairs your judgment, but not your reaction time.
C. It impairs your reaction time and your decision-making.
D. It impairs your vision but not your driving skills.

Correct Answer is C. It impairs your reaction time and your decision-making. Alcohol lowers your reflexes, vision, judgment of distance, alertness, and every other driving skill.

40. What should you do when driving into a work zone?

A. Turn on cruise control.
B. Shorten your following distance so traffic can move more freely.
C. Lengthen your following distance.
D. It depends on the road conditions.

Correct Answer is C. Lengthen your following distance. Stay further from the car in front of you so you have more time to react.

41. Your light turns green. However, the traffic in front of you is backed up into the intersection. What should you do?

    A. Move ahead slowly and stop behind the last car.
    B. Make a U-turn so you can get back to the turn when it's clear.
    C. Merge into the adjacent lane so you can get around the traffic.
    D. Stay stopped at the green light until the traffic clears out of the intersection.

Correct Answer is D. Stay stopped at the green light until the traffic clears out of the intersection.

42. Your car starts to skid, with the rear end turning to the left. What should you do?

    A. Steer left
    B. Steer right
    C. Slam the brakes
    D. Slam the gas

Correct Answer is A. Steer left. If your car is in a skid, don't accelerate or brake. Slowly steer in the direction the car can safely go.

43. Define "too slow" in terms of your vehicle's driving speed.

    A. Too far below the speed limit
    B. When cars start honking at you
    C. When you're blocking other cars
    D. When everyone else is going faster

Correct Answer is C. When you're blocking other cars. The speed of other cars doesn't matter because they could be driving unsafely. Under normal conditions, "too slow" means you are blocking other drivers who are driving normally.

44. Why do some speed limit signs have a minimum speed?

    A. To catch people speeding
    B. To keep traffic flowing
    C. To prevent speeding past obstacles
    D. To slow down traffic on crowded streets

Correct Answer is B. To keep traffic flowing. Speed minimums prevent vehicles from blocking the road.

45. At a traffic circle, which cars should you yield to?

    A. Cars in the circle already
    B. Cars entering the circle now
    C. Cars exiting the circle
    D. Cars trying to pass you in the adjacent lane

Correct Answer is A. Cars in the circle already. Vehicles in a traffic circle have no signal to stop and do not have to yield. Cars outside the circle must yield to them before entering.

46. Look in all directions before passing a stopped school bus with its lights flashing.

    A. True
    B. False

Correct Answer is B. False. Never pass a stopped school bus when its signal lights are flashing.

47. When making a right turn at a red light, what should you do?

    A. Speed up and signal the turn as you go.
    B. Change lanes as fast as possible.
    C. Stop first.
    D. Drive at a normal speed.

Correct Answer is C. Stop first. When making a right turn, yield to cars in the lane you're turning into and proceed when it's clear.

48. What is true of most crashes around a work zone?

    A. They are rear-end collisions.
    B. They are T-bone accidents.
    C. They happen at night.
    D. They result in injured workers.

Correct Answer is A. They are rear-end collisions. Not paying close attention to the speed of the other cars in the work zone is the most common cause of these accidents.

49. When railroad crossings have no signage or signals and no clear visibility down the tracks, what should your speed limit be?

    A. 35 mph
    B. 25 mph
    C. 15 mph
    D. 5 mph

Correct Answer is C. 15 mph.

50. When the road is marked with a broken yellow line next to a solid yellow line, cars on that road:

    A. May pass when driving next to the solid line.
    B. May pass when driving next to the broken line.
    C. May pass on either side of the line.
    D. May never pass over the line.

Correct Answer is B. May pass when driving next to the broken line. Only vehicles on that side of the road may pass.

51. Hydroplaning results in drivers losing control over their cars on wet roads. What causes hydroplaning?

    A. Stopping too frequently
    B. Stopping too suddenly
    C. Driving too slowly
    D. Driving too fast

Correct Answer is D. Driving too fast. Hydroplaning is far more likely to occur when cars drive too fast for the current road conditions.

52. When passing another car:

    A. Assume the other car will drive normally.
    B. Assume the other car will slow down.
    C. Assume the other car sees you.
    D. Assume the other car doesn't see you.

Correct Answer is D. Assume the other car doesn't see you. When passing proceed with caution; you can't rely on the other car's behavior.

53. The speed limit is always the maximum safe speed to drive.

    A. True
    B. False

Correct Answer is B. False. Weather and road conditions can change the maximum safe driving speed.

54. When driving on a road with multiple lanes, what do you do if another driver cuts you off?

    A. Remain calm and slow down if necessary.
    B. Remain calm and cautiously speed up to pass the other car.
    C. Stop completely and take a deep breath.
    D. Honk your horn and turn into another lane.

Correct Answer is A. Remain calm and slow down if necessary. Take stock of your surroundings and avoid collisions by staying calm and slowing down where appropriate.

55. How should you get home after attending a social event and having a few drinks?

    A. Plan ahead of time to drive on roads with no traffic late at night, just to be safe.
    B. Make sure you drive extra slowly to compensate for your impaired vision.
    C. Use a taxi, Uber driver, or a friend that agrees not to drink to take you home.
    D. Stay at the event until you feel safe to get behind the wheel.

Correct Answer is C. Use a taxi, Uber driver, or a friend that agrees not to drink to take you home. Don't get in a car after drinking unless a registered public transportation driver or a friend who has not been drinking is behind the wheel.

56. If your car has anti-lock brakes (ABS) and you need to make a quick stop on a slippery road, what should you do?

    A. Slam the brake, hold it down, and steer.
    B. Pump the brake carefully while steering to prevent skidding.
    C. Pump the brake hard and fast while steering to prevent skidding.
    D. Slam the brake once, release it, and steer out of danger.

Correct Answer is A. Slam the brake, hold it down, and steer. With ABS, you need to push the brake down, hold it down, and steer the car out of danger.

57. Other than your driver's license, what document will a police officer most likely ask you to give them if they stop you on the road?

    A. Social security card
    B. Insurance card
    C. Registration card
    D. Working VISA

Correct Answer is C. Registration card. The officer needs to be able to connect you to the car you're driving, so they'll ask for your license and registration if they pull you over.

58. What color flags mark a load that sticks out of a vehicle more than four feet from the back?

    A. White
    B. Blue
    C. Yellow
    D. Red

Correct Answer is D. Red. Four red flags denote a projecting load during the daytime.

59. What do signs shaped like upside-down triangles mean?

    A. Stop
    B. Yield
    C. Do not enter
    D. Slow down

Correct Answer is B. Yield. Watch for other cars and pedestrians depending on the situation.

60. Unless a speed limit sign says otherwise, what is the most common speed limit for cars in residential areas?

    A. 15 mph
    B. 20 mph
    C. 25 mph
    D. 30 mph

Correct Answer is D. 30 mph. Watch for kids playing and pay attention to posted speed limits. If there aren't any, 30 mph is standard for residential areas.

61. When can you use a three-point turn on a public road?

    A. Any time U-turns are allowed as well, but the road is too narrow for them
    B. Any time the road curves, so long as there's no hill
    C. Any time a U-turn is prohibited due to a sign at the corner
    D. Any time you can

Correct Answer is A. Any time U-turns are allowed as well, but the road is too narrow for them.

62. What is the minimum legal distance you can park from a fire hydrant?

    A. 10 feet
    B. 15 feet
    C. 20 feet
    D. 25 feet

Correct Answer is B. 15 feet.

63. The passenger not wearing their seat belt receives the seat belt violation if they're less than 17 years old when the car is pulled over.

    A. True
    B. False

Correct Answer is B. False. The driver receives the seat belt violation if their underage passengers aren't buckled up.

64. If you are in a crash and don't have any vehicle insurance:

    A. You will be arrested.
    B. You will be required to attend safety seminars.
    C. You may have your license suspended and have to pay damages/fees to reinstate it.
    D. You may have to serve prison time.

Correct Answer is C. You may have your license suspended and pay damages/fees to reinstate it.

65. If you are driving at night, you can use your parking lights instead of headlights:

    A. All the time.
    B. When the road is clear.
    C. When driving in residential areas.
    D. Never.

Correct Answer is D. Never. Parking lights can never legally be used instead of headlights.

66. What should you do when you see a driver displaying signs of road rage, such as swearing, swerving, or cutting off other drivers?

    A. Turn off the road as fast as possible.
    B. Yell and honk your horn.
    C. Drive cautiously and slow down where possible.
    D. Drive cautiously and try to get ahead of them.

Correct Answer is C. Drive cautiously and slow down where possible. Don't try to overtake an angry driver. Slow down and let them pass you.

67. What is the maximum number of drinks a designated driver can have?

    A. 0
    B. 1
    C. 2
    D. 3

Correct Answer is A. 0. A designated driver cannot consume any alcohol. They are responsible for getting everyone else home safely from the social event.

68. Single broken yellow lines mean:

    A. You can drive in either lane.
    B. You can drive left of the line and pass when safe.
    C. You can drive left of the line but never pass.
    D. You can never cross the line.

Correct Answer is B. You can drive left of the line and pass when safe.

69. What is a reversible lane?

    A. Traffic can go in either direction all the time.
    B. Traffic is always reversed.
    C. Traffic can reverse direction at certain times of day.
    D. Traffic can only move backward.

Correct Answer is C. Traffic can reverse direction at certain times of the day. Marked by arrows, signs, or signals, reversible lanes can change direction to accommodate rush-hour traffic.

70. You must yield to pedestrians at a crosswalk:

    A. All the time.
    B. Only when they have the right of way.
    C. Only when their signal is green.
    D. Only when you come to a stop sign.

Correct Answer is A. All the time. Pedestrians always have the right of way. The traffic signals are for their safety, not the drivers' permission. Always proceed with caution around crosswalks and yield to pedestrians.

71. If your car has an automatic transmission, what should you do when you park on a hill?

    A. Shift into Park and then pull the parking brake.
    B. Shift into Park and don't pull the parking brake.
    C. Pull the parking brake and don't shift into Park.
    D. Pull the parking brake and then shift into Park.

Correct Answer is D. Pull the parking brake and then shift into Park. Pulling the brake first prevents you from sliding down the hill.

72. If a police officer suspects that your car is not being maintained properly, how much notice are they required to give you before inspecting it?

    A. They can inspect it at any time.
    B. They must give 10 days' notice.
    C. They must give 2 weeks' notice.
    D. They can never inspect your car.

Correct Answer is A. They can inspect it any time. If they suspect your car isn't up to code, they are allowed to pull you over at any time and inspect it.

73. If there is no bicycle lane, where are cyclists legally allowed to ride?

    A. Middle of the lane
    B. Close to the right shoulder
    C. Close to the left shoulder
    D. Cyclists are not allowed on roads without bicycle lanes.

Correct Answer is B. Close to the right shoulder. Cyclists should stay on the road, but as far from the middle of the lane as possible.

74. Drivers under the age of 17 cannot operate a motor vehicle without being accompanied by a legal adult during what time of day?

    A. 12 am to 7 am
    B. 11 pm to 6 am
    C. 3 am to 8 am
    D. 8 am to 5 pm

Correct Answer is B. 11 pm to 6 am. An exception is when the young driver must drive during this time to or from work.

75. When may you legally park in front of a driveway?

    A. If it's your driveway
    B. If you won't be there longer than 10 minutes
    C. If it's nighttime
    D. Never

Correct Answer is D. Never.

76. When you are about to make a left-hand turn, when should you yield to other cars?

    A. Never
    B. Always, unless they're making a right turn
    C. Until you don't see too many coming
    D. Until you can turn safely

Correct Answer is D. Until you can turn safely. You shouldn't have to accelerate or brake quickly, or force other cars to do so, during a left-hand turn. You must wait until it's safe.

77. When your entrance lane onto a busy highway is very short, such as after a tollbooth, what is the safest way to drive onto the highway?

    A. Reduce your speed and proceed cautiously into traffic.
    B. Turn harder so you can get into the gap between cars.
    C. Stop and wait for a gap in the traffic, then accelerate quickly.
    D. Accelerate in the entrance lane so other drivers see you.

Correct Answer is C. Stop and wait for a gap in the traffic, then accelerate quickly.

78. You have the right of way. What should you do?

    A. Honk before driving carefully.
    B. Drive normally, but carefully.
    C. Wait at the intersection until all other cars are gone.
    D. Stop for a few seconds before turning into the intersection.

Correct Answer is B. Drive normally, but carefully. If you have the right of way, you don't have to stop, honk, or wait.

79. Large trucks on the road have:

    A. Smaller blind spots than normal cars.
    B. Longer stopping times than normal cars.
    C. To make shallow turns.
    D. Both A and B

Correct Answer is B. Longer stopping times than normal cars. Blind spots are even larger for trucks than for normal cars, and they must take turns very wide sometimes crossing into other lanes.

80. If you back up your car, you should:

    A. Back up slowly.
    B. Honk your horn.
    C. Turn to the left to see behind you.
    D. Focus on your mirrors to see behind you.

Correct Answer is A. Back up slowly.

81. You have a right to your driver's license.

    A. True
    B. False

Correct Answer is B. False. Having a driver's license is not a legal right. It is a privilege depending on many factors.

82. If you cross an intersection and are about to turn into a driveway, when should you signal?

    A. Never
    B. As long as possible
    C. Before you're in the intersection
    D. After you're in the intersection

Correct Answer is D. After you're in the intersection. If you signal too early, cars behind you may think you're turning at the intersection rather than the driveway.

83. Can you turn right at a red light without stopping?

    A. No.
    B. Yes, so long as no sign says otherwise.
    C. Yes, so long as there are no cars coming.
    D. Yes, always.

Correct Answer is A. No. You must stop at a red light before turning right checking to see if the turn is legal and safe.

84. The sides of the highway are marked by solid white lines. When is it legal to cross them?

    A. When traffic is backed up and you want to get off the road
    B. When you want to pass a stopped car
    C. When other cars are all crossing the line
    D. When your car breaks down

Correct Answer is D. When your car breaks down. If you need to pull off the road for safety reasons, it is legal to cross the white line on a highway.

85. Solid yellow lines separate:

    A. Traffic moving in one direction.
    B. Traffic on one-way roads.
    C. Traffic moving in both directions.
    D. Traffic lanes and bicycle lanes.

Correct Answer is C. Traffic moving in both directions.

86. You reach an intersection and stop at a red light. A police officer in the road signals you to proceed. What should you do?

    A. Tell the police officer that the light is red.
    B. Wait until the light turns green.
    C. Listen to the police officer and proceed.
    D. Stop and look around to make sure it's safe.

Correct Answer is C. Listen to the police officer and proceed. It's their job to make sure the lanes are safe. Proceed when the police officer signals without stopping.

87. If you are in a car crash, which of these things should you NOT do?

    A. Help injured passengers.
    B. Drive home and call the police.
    C. Exchange insurance information with the other driver.
    D. Stop your car.

Correct Answer is B. Drive home and call the police. Notify the police and your insurance company from the site. You cannot drive home until they make a report.

88. If you turn left onto a two-way road, what lane should you turn into?

    A. The right lane
    B. The center lane
    C. The left lane
    D. It doesn't matter

Correct Answer is C. The left lane. Turn into the lane closest to the lane that you are turning from and to the right of the yellow line, in this case, the left lane.

89. Solid white lines on the highway can be legally crossed:

    A. When you need to make a U-turn.
    B. When you need to turn into a driveway.
    C. When the traffic requires you to do so.
    D. When you want to go faster.

Correct Answer is C. When the traffic requires you to do so. You can pass or change lanes over a solid white line, but only if road conditions make it necessary.

90. Where should your wheels be turned when you park uphill on a street with two lanes and no curb?

    A. Toward the side of the road
    B. Toward the street
    C. Parallel to the street
    D. Whichever direction is most convenient

Correct Answer is A. Toward the side of the road. If your car is parked uphill, you want to turn your wheels to the right, toward where the curb would be.

91. What should you do when you hear a siren while driving?

    A. Slow down and look around for the emergency vehicle.
    B. Speed up to get out of the vehicle's way.
    C. Continue driving normally and let the vehicle pass.
    D. Pull over and look to see if the vehicle is on your street.

Correct Answer is D. Pull over and look to see if the vehicle is on your street. Getting out of the way of the emergency vehicle is the most important thing.

92. Your brake pedal drops to the floor of your car. What should you do?

    A. Pump the pedal until it rises back up.
    B. Turn the car off and call a mechanic.
    C. Push it up from below with the top of your foot.
    D. Pull the emergency brake.

Correct Answer is A. Pump the pedal until it rises back up. You may be able to build the brake pressure back up if you pump it gently.

93. What should you turn on when your car breaks down on the road?

    A. Your four-way flashers
    B. Your horn
    C. Your high-beam headlights
    D. Your low-beam headlights

Correct Answer is A. Your four-way flashers. This warns other drivers to safely pass you.

94. What signal can direct drivers on the highway into their new turn lanes?

    A. Flashing yellow lights
    B. Flashing red lights
    C. Flashing green lights
    D. White arrows on the road

Correct Answer is D. White arrows on the road. White arrows can direct drivers to the lanes they should be using to turn.

95. What time of day can you practice driving with a learner's permit?

    A. 12 pm to 9 pm
    B. 5 am to 11 pm
    C. 12 am to 8 am
    D. 9 am to 5 pm

Correct Answer is B. 5 am to 11 pm.

96. A school bus flashes its red lights. You should:

    A. Stop right behind the bus.
    B. Slow down and watch for kids.
    C. Stop 25 feet from the bus.
    D. Speed up to get around the bus.

Correct Answer is C. Stop 25 feet from the bus. Never pass a bus when its lights are flashing.

97. When turning left at an intersection where you have a green light but traffic is heavy:

   A. Turn at the next intersection.
   B. Wait in the intersection until you have space to turn.
   C. Take your right of way and let the other drivers react.
   D. Stop in the crosswalk until the other cars are gone.

Correct Answer is B. Wait in the intersection until you have space to turn. You can't turn until the intersection is clear.

98. Signs shaped like rectangles tell you:
   A. The road is turning in one direction.
   B. To slow down in school zones.
   C. The speed limit.
   D. Both A and C

Correct Answer is D. Both A and C. Rectangular signs could indicate either speed limits or one-directional turns.

99. If you see the line on the right side of the highway slant into the lane to the left, what does this mean?

    A. There's a left turn coming up.
    B. There's an intersection coming up.
    C. The road is narrower up ahead.
    D. The road is under construction up ahead.

Correct Answer is C. The road is narrower up ahead.

100. What should you do before you turn?

    A. Signal
    B. Slow down
    C. Speed up
    D. Both A and B

Correct Answer is D. Both A and B.

101. At an intersection, a pedestrian is crossing the road without a traffic signal. A driver is trying to make a right-hand turn. Who should yield in this situation?

    A. The pedestrian
    B. The driver
    C. Whoever started crossing first
    D. Whoever is on the right

Correct Answer is B. The driver. Cars must always yield to pedestrians.

102. When the road is wet, your tires:

    A. Are less effective.
    B. Are more effective.
    C. Are unaffected.
    D. Are less prone to slipping.

Correct Answer is A. Are less effective. Water forms a thin layer between your tires and the road that reduces traction and makes your tires less effective.

103. When exiting parking spaces that lie parallel to the curb, make sure you first:

    A. Turn on your flashers.
    B. Honk your horn.
    C. Check for traffic in your rear-view mirror.
    D. Check for traffic by looking.

Correct Answer is D. Check for traffic by looking. When exiting a parallel parking space, turn your head to check for traffic. Don't rely on your mirrors.

104. When a sign says, "do not enter," it means that the road:

    A. Is a restricted roadway.
    B. Is closed for construction.
    C. Is a highway exit.
    D. Is a pedestrian crossing.

Correct Answer is A. Is a restricted roadway. Normal traffic cannot use this road.

105. When are U-turns legal in residential areas?

    A. When you're driving on a one-way street
    B. When no vehicles are approaching
    C. When a sign says you can make U-turns
    D. When the road is marked with double yellow lines

Correct Answer is B. When no vehicles are approaching. There are no road markings that will tell you to make U-turns in residential districts. Watch for traffic and proceed cautiously.

106. When you are caught driving under the influence, you:

    A. Have to pay a $100 fine.
    B. Have your license suspended for 5 years.
    C. Have to spend at least 12 hours in jail, depending on the amount of alcohol you consumed.
    D. Have to attend Alcohol Highway Safety School.

Correct Answer is D. Have to attend Alcohol Highway Safety School.

107. On one-way streets, you can only turn left when:

    A. Traffic moves to the left.
    B. Traffic moves to the right.
    C. A sign shows you where to turn.
    D. No other cars are on the road.

Correct Answer is A. Traffic moves to the left. You can only turn left if traffic is going in that direction.

108. On wet roads, you should change your following distance:

    A. To 2 seconds.
    B. To 6 seconds.
    C. To 4 seconds like normal.
    D. To 10 seconds just to be safe.

Correct Answer is B. To 6 seconds. You need to increase your following distance by about 50% from normal when the roads are wet.

109. People under the age of 21 cannot:

    A. Possess alcohol.
    B. Serve alcohol.
    C. Be with someone drinking alcohol.
    D. Advertise alcohol.

Correct Answer is A. Possess alcohol. People under the age of 21 can serve at restaurants, so the other options are legal under the right circumstances.

110. Double solid yellow lines can only be passed when:

    A. The driver in front of you is moving 15 miles under the speed limit or more.
    B. Traffic is low enough to pass safely.
    C. You need to turn into a driveway.
    D. The weather conditions are safe.

Correct Answer is C. You need to turn into a driveway.

111. When a sign says, "no stopping," and there's no police officer directing traffic, you can only stop:

    A. If you need to unload passengers.
    B. If you're making a delivery.
    C. If you'll only be there for five minutes or less.
    D. If you need to avoid traffic.

Correct Answer is D. If you need to avoid traffic. You should never stop at No Stopping signs unless it would make you conflict with the oncoming traffic.

112. When a car looks like it's going to hit you, get their attention with:

    A. Your horn.
    B. Your voice.
    C. Your arms.
    D. Your headlights.

Correct Answer is A. Your horn.

113. When driving on snow or ice:

    A. Speed up to increase traction and reduce your chance of slipping.

    B. Slow down to avoid sudden stops.

    C. Use your lights and horn to stay safe.

    D. Shorten your following distance.

Correct Answer is B. Slow down to avoid sudden stops. Icy roads are most dangerous when you must make sudden turns or stops because you're going too fast.

114. If you are underage and a police officer asks you to take a breath, blood, or urine test, you:

    A. May refuse due to your age.

    B. Must sign a consent form before taking the test.

    C. May choose which test you would prefer to take.

    D. Must listen to the officer and take the test.

Correct Answer is D. Must listen to the officer and take the test. Otherwise, you will have your license suspended.

115. What happens when you tailgate other drivers?

    A. You look really tough
    B. You help reduce traffic by shortening the following distance
    C. You agitate other drivers
    D. You get to your destination quicker

Correct Answer is C. You agitate other drivers. Tailgating, or driving too close to the bumper of the driver in front of you, can agitate the other driver and make an accident more likely.

116. Pentagonal signs (signs with five sides) with two people on them indicate:

    A. An intersection.
    B. A crosswalk.
    C. A pedestrians-only lane.
    D. A school crossing.

Correct Answer is D. A school crossing. Adjust your speed accordingly.

117. Taking your hands off the wheel:

    A. Is okay when you're eating.
    B. Is okay when you're showing off.
    C. Is okay if you're a good enough driver.
    D. Is never okay.

Correct Answer is D. Is never okay. Taking your hands off the wheel reduces your ability to react to danger and avoid collisions.

118. You should always keep your eyes straight ahead without moving when driving on a highway.

    A. True
    B. False

Correct Answer is B. False. Your eyes should be moving within your field of view to check your following distance, road signs, and the behavior of other drivers.

119. When you can't see other vehicles from _____ feet away, you have to turn on your headlights.

    A. 500
    B. 1000
    C. 1500
    D. 2000

Correct Answer is B. 1000.

120. After passing a car, return to your original lane only when:

    A. You know that the other car has seen your signal.
    B. Your headlights are on.
    C. The other car signals with their headlights.
    D. You can see their bumper in your rearview mirror.

Correct Answer is D. You can see their bumper in your rearview mirror.

121. When children are playing nearby, you can expect them to:

    A. Stop when they see your car.
    B. Stay on the sidewalk.
    C. Know the rules of the road.
    D. Run in front of your car.

Correct Answer is D. Run in front of your car. Always expect that children don't see you.

122. Lack of sleep affects your driving similarly to:

    A. Alcohol.
    B. Anger.
    C. Blindness.
    D. Drugs.

Correct Answer is A. Alcohol. Your judgment is similarly impaired when you haven't gotten enough sleep as when you've had too many drinks.

123. When taking medication while drinking alcohol, the combination can:

    A. Increase the effectiveness of the medication.
    B. Decrease the effectiveness of the medication.
    C. Increase the effects of the alcohol.
    D. Decrease the effects of the alcohol.

Correct Answer is C. Increase the effects of the alcohol.

124. When you see a sign with a straight arrow pointing down next to a straight arrow pointing up, you know that the traffic ahead:

    A. Is approaching an intersection.
    B. Is approaching a divided highway.
    C. Is using all four lanes.
    D. Is traveling in both directions.

Correct Answer is D. Is traveling in both directions.

125. Teenagers show a statistically higher chance of being in an accident when they drive:

    A. With other teenagers.
    B. With their pets.
    C. With adults.
    D. Without anyone else in the car.

Correct Answer is A. With other teenagers.

126. When you see that a traffic light isn't working, you should:

    A. Yield to other traffic just to be safe.
    B. Stop, look around, and proceed cautiously.
    C. Drive normally unless traffic is too busy.
    D. Turn off the road before you get to the light.

Correct Answer is B. Stop, look around, and proceed cautiously. Treat traffic lights that aren't working similarly to stop signs.

127. When driving in rain, make sure you:

    A. Drive faster to escape the rain.
    B. Increase your following distance.
    C. Decrease your following distance.
    D. Both A and B

Correct Answer is B. Increase your following distance. When the roads are wet, stopping quickly becomes more difficult. Increase your following distance to stay safe.

128. What is the white line painted on the road at the intersection called?

    A. Turn lane line
    B. Crosswalk
    C. Limit line
    D. Highway divider

Correct Answer is C. Limit line. This is the closest to the intersection your car should be.

129. The safest response to hydroplaning is to:

    A. Slam the brakes.
    B. Pump the brakes.
    C. Gradually slow down.
    D. Accelerate.

Correct Answer is C. Gradually slow down. You don't want to use the brakes when your car starts to hydroplane.

130. At a through road, you come to an intersection without any signs telling you to stop or yield. You should:

    A. Stay with traffic.
    B. Yield to traffic.
    C. Turn because you have the right of way.
    D. Stop just to be safe.

Correct Answer is B. Yield to traffic. When approaching an intersection with no signage, yield to ongoing traffic as well as bicycles and pedestrians.

131. When the highway is marked by a solid white line, you should:

    A. Pass whenever you need to.
    B. Watch for traffic moving in the opposite direction.
    C. Stay in your lane.
    D. Feel free to do U-turns.

Correct Answer is C. Stay in your lane. Unless something happens that requires you to switch lanes, stay in one lane.

132. Double yellow solid lines with more than two feet of space between them indicate:

    A. One-way traffic.
    B. Two-way traffic.
    C. The borders of a parking lot.
    D. A barrier.

Correct Answer is D. A barrier. These lines indicate that cars should not cross these lines.

133. When you hear an emergency vehicle's siren while you're passing through an intersection, what should you do?

    A. Drive through the intersection normally, then pull to the right and stop.

    B. Drive through the intersection normally, then pull to the left and stop.

    C. Wait at the intersection for the vehicle to pass.

    D. Turn at the intersection instead to get off the road.

Correct Answer is A. Drive through the intersection normally, then pull to the right and stop.

134. Solid double white lines on the road indicate:

    A. Lanes moving in different directions where you cannot pass.

    B. Lanes moving in the same direction where you can pass.

    C. Lanes moving in the same direction where you cannot pass.

    D. Lanes moving in different directions where you can pass.

Correct Answer is C. Lanes moving in the same direction where you cannot pass.

135. To see in intense fog, turn on your:

    A. Low-beams.
    B. High-beams.
    C. Four-way flashers.
    D. Emergency signal.

Correct Answer is A. Low-beams. Drive slowly while using your low-beam headlights to see without causing a glare.

136. When your car seems to be having mechanical trouble and you need to stop, first you should:

    A. Open your hood.
    B. Stop immediately.
    C. Pull off the road.
    D. Turn on your emergency flashers.

Correct Answer is C. Pull off the road. Get away from traffic, and THEN turn on your emergency flashers to signal to traffic that you're having mechanical issues.

137. If you are involved in a collision with another car, what is the maximum amount of time you can wait to notify your local DMV?

    A. 10 days
    B. 15 days
    C. 20 days
    D. 1 month

Correct Answer is A. 10 days.

138. When the backseats of your car are occupied by children younger than 7, another young child may:

    A. Sit in someone's lap so long as they have a seatbelt.
    B. Sit in the front seat so long as they have a seat belt.
    C. Sit wherever they want.
    D. Both A and B

Correct Answer is B. Sit in the front seat so long as they have a seat belt.

139. How many feet will your car continue to travel after slamming on the brake when you're driving at 60 mph?

    A. 200
    B. 300
    C. 400
    D. 500

Correct Answer is C. 400.

140. If your parked car rolls and hits another car in the parking lot, what should you do?

    A. Search for the car's owner.
    B. Call the police.
    C. Drive away.
    D. Honk your horn until the other driver comes.

Correct Answer is B. Call the police. Like any accident, this situation needs to be reported immediately.

141. Octagonal signs always mean you should:

    A. Yield
    B. Stop
    C. Turn
    D. Speed up

Correct Answer is B. Stop.

142. On a normal two-lane highway, how fast can you drive while towing a trailer?

    A. 55 mph
    B. 45 mph
    C. 65 mph
    D. 25 mph

Correct Answer is A. 55 mph. Unless otherwise posted by signs, this is the maximum speed a car towing a trailer can travel on a two-lane undivided highway.

143. Flashing yellow arrows mean you should:

    A. Stop.
    B. Yield.
    C. Turn a different direction.
    D. Do a U-turn.

Correct Answer is B. Yield. At a flashing yellow light, yield to traffic and drive cautiously in the direction of the arrow.

144. When an officer signals for you to pull over, what's the first thing you should do?

    A. Stop at the median.
    B. Pull over to the side of the road.
    C. Turn on your emergency flashers.
    D. Turn on your right turn signal.

Correct Answer is D. Turn on your right turn signal. This tells the officer that you've seen him and you're preparing to safely turn off the road to the right.

145. If a crosswalk is unmarked, what should you do?

    A. Accelerate to get through before pedestrians cross.

    B. Yell at pedestrians to move faster.

    C. Move cautiously through the crosswalk to avoid hitting anyone.

    D. Yield to any pedestrians in the crosswalk.

Correct Answer is D. Yield to any pedestrians in the crosswalk.

146. When you see a sign with a black arrow pointing forward and another arrow curving to the left, this means you should:

    A. Merge to the left on the road ahead.

    B. Decide to turn left or go straight.

    C. Go straight and watch for traffic moving to the left.

    D. Turn as soon as possible to avoid a one-way road ahead.

Correct Answer is B. Decide to turn left or go straight. This sign means that the road ahead both turns and continues in the current direction.

147. Before making a safe, legal turn, first you should:

    A. Accelerate.

    B. Decelerate.

    C. Adjust your mirrors.

    D. Move into the proper lane.

Correct Answer is D. Move into the proper lane. Well before you need to make the turn, you should be in the lane on the side of the road you wish to turn onto.

148. Regulatory devices on the road always help you see:

    A. Where to stop, where to turn, and what speed to drive.

    B. Where the hazards are, where the road changes elevation, and where workers are.

    C. Where to stop for construction and where to make proper turns.

    D. How fast you're going and where to stop for pedestrians.

Correct Answer is A. Where to stop, where to turn, and what speed to drive. Regulatory devices like signs and traffic controls tell you what to DO, whereas other types of signs tell you about things that are physically on the road, like workers.

149. If your car breaks down and you must leave it on the road, you should never:

    A. Turn it off.
    B. Turn the parking brake on.
    C. Lock the ignition.
    D. Roll the windows down.

Correct Answer is D. Roll the windows down. You should do everything else, but make sure the windows are rolled up if you must leave your car.

150. A diamond-shaped sign with the silhouette of one person on it indicates:

    A. A work zone up ahead.
    B. A crosswalk up ahead.
    C. A flagger up ahead.
    D. A school zone up ahead.

Correct Answer is B. A crosswalk up ahead. Prepare to yield to pedestrians.

151. Many traffic lanes have a wide white line marked on the road just before an intersection. This is called the limit line and tells you where you must:

    A. Stop for a signal or stop sign.
    B. Stop to allow pedestrians to use the crosswalk.
    C. Stop to yield to drivers in a roundabout.
    D. Slow down before turning.

Correct Answers is A. Stop for a signal or stop sign. These lines mark intersections and help you see where to stop out of the way of traffic in the other lanes.

152. When using your headlights, you should never:

    A. Use low-beams while driving in busy cities.
    B. Use high-beams while driving close behind other cars.
    C. Use low-beams while driving in the rain.
    D. Use high-beams to signal someone to move.

Correct Answer is B. Use high-beams while driving close behind other cars. This can disorient and distract the cars in front of you. Only use high-beams when driving at night with no oncoming traffic.

153. If a car driving toward you has its high-beam headlights on, you could become temporarily blinded. This is why you should look toward:

    A. The oncoming car.
    B. The center of the road.
    C. The right edge of the road.
    D. The left edge of the road.

Correct Answer is C. The right edge of the road. This will help you steer if your vision is disoriented for a moment.

154. Yielding on a road means:

    A. Slowing down and being prepared to stop.
    B. Slowing down and being prepared to turn.
    C. Speeding up and being prepared to turn.
    D. Speeding up and watching for pedestrians.

Correct Answer is A. Slowing down and being prepared to stop. When yielding, often marked by a sign, watch for pedestrians or other vehicles, and prepare to stop to allow them to pass.

155. What kind of road is the most dangerous in terms of collisions between cars and motorcycles?

    A. Highways
    B. Dark city roads
    C. Roundabouts
    D. Intersections

Correct Answer is D. Intersections. This is the most likely place a car will not see a motorcycle's path.

156. As you enter a roundabout, you will always enter the circle to the:

    A. Right.
    B. Left.
    C. Center.

Correct Answer is A. Right. Roundabouts are entered to the right and travel in a counterclockwise direction.

157. Use high-beam headlights:

    A. Whenever it rains.
    B. Whenever there's heavy fog.
    C. Whenever it's dark on country or city roads.
    D. Whenever your visibility is low and traffic is high.

Correct Answer is C. Whenever it's dark on country or city roads.

158. If your car breaks down on a narrow highway that has no side of the road to turn off onto, what should you do?

    A. Wait inside your car on the road.
    B. Get out of the car and flag down some help.
    C. Push the car to the nearest exit.
    D. Get out on the passenger's side and walk to safety.

Correct Answer is D. Get out on the passenger's side and walk to safety. On high-speed roads, drivers in broken-down vehicles are in danger. They should exit on the side of the road's edge and walk to a safe place.

159. If you see a high-occupancy vehicle lane, you can only use it when:

    A. You are driving farm equipment.
    B. Your trailer contains more than 4 people.
    C. You are driving a carpool.
    D. You are driving a bus.

Correct Answer is C. You are driving a carpool. With more than one person in a carpool vehicle, you can use lanes restricted for HOVs.

160. If you see another driver using their cellphone while at the wheel, what should you do?

    A. Call the police.
    B. Increase your following distance.
    C. Honk to get their attention.
    D. Turn off the road for your own safety.

Correct Answer is B. Increase your following distance. It's not your business to report them to the police and use your phone in the process. Drive carefully and increase your distance from them so you can react if something happens.

161. On a two-lane road, what should you do when you try to pass a bicycle at the same time an oncoming car is approaching?

    A. Accelerate to get past the bicycle quickly.
    B. Gauge the space to make sure the oncoming car has room as you pass.
    C. Slow down and let the car pass first.
    D. Turn off the road just to be safe.

Correct Answer is C. Slow down and let the car pass first. At that point, you'll have plenty of room to pass the bicycle.

162. A sign with an arrow and the word "only" is a reminder that:

    A. You should keep your eyes forward.
    B. You can only go straight.
    C. You are approaching a one-way street.
    D. You are approaching a street with one lane.

Correct Answer is B. You can only go straight. Vehicles are not allowed to turn on this road.

163. Which of these statements is true?

    A. Both kinds of headlights are equally useful in fog.
    B. High-beams are useful in fog.
    C. Low-beams are useful in fog.
    D. Both kinds of headlights are equally not useful in fog.

Correct Answer is C. Low-beams are useful in fog. High-beams cause reflections that do not aid visibility in fog.

164. When traffic moves in opposite directions, the lanes are divided by:

    A. Black lines.
    B. Yellow lines.
    C. White lines.
    D. Blue lines.

Correct Answer is B. Yellow lines.

165. When traffic moves in the same direction, the lanes are divided by:

  A. Black lines.
  B. Yellow lines.
  C. White lines.
  D. Blue lines.

Correct Answer is C. White lines.

166. When you want to pass a vehicle, when should you signal?

  A. 500 feet before passing
  B. When you're ready to pass
  C. Right when you start passing
  D. After you begin to pass

Correct Answer is B. When you're ready to pass. Signaling too early or late can confuse other drivers and make it hard for them to give you room.

167. When you see signs with electronic arrows on them, a work zone is telling you to:

    A. Use the parking zone it's pointing to.
    B. Turn off at the intersection it's pointing to.
    C. Drive in the lanes it's pointing to.
    D. Avoid the hazard it's pointing to.

Correct Answer is C. Drive in the lanes it's pointing to. These signs are used to direct drivers through work zones by telling which lanes to use.

168. When traffic travels in opposite directions, what is a center lane used for?

    A. Making left turns
    B. Making right turns
    C. Passing other cars
    D. Making U-turns

Correct Answer is A. Making left turns. This is called a center left-turn lane.

169. Tailgating while driving means:

    A. Listening to a football game.
    B. Driving too close to other cars.
    C. Passing without signaling.
    D. Honking behind other cars.

Correct Answer is B. Driving too close to other cars. Tailgating increases the likelihood of rear-end collisions.

170. As you back up your car, make sure to look in front of you, behind, and to the sides. Then, while backing up, you should keep looking:

    A. To the left side.
    B. To the right side.
    C. To the front.
    D. To the back.

Correct Answer is D. To the back. Make sure to keep your head turned around while backing up.

171. Airbags are always:

    A. Installed in every car.
    B. Installed instead of seat belts.
    C. On both the driver's and passenger's side.
    D. Intended to add to the safety of seat belts.

Correct Answer is D. Intended to add to the safety of seat belts. Airbags should not replace a seat belt—they should provide an additional safety measure.

172. When you exit a high-speed highway onto a slower road with traffic behind you:

    A. Speed up.
    B. Slow down.
    C. Try to speed up gradually.
    D. Try not to slow down too quickly.

Correct Answer is D. Try not to slow down too quickly. Let the traffic behind you gradually match your new speed. Sudden changes lead to greater chances of collision.

173. If another driver is tailgating you, you should:

    A. Speed up to get away from them.
    B. Slow down to force them to pass.
    C. Change lanes to let them pass.
    D. Turn off the road to avoid a collision.

Correct Answer is C. Change lanes to let them pass. Aggressive drivers are best dealt with by staying calm, not by an aggressive solution.

174. Use high-beam headlights:

    A. To see in the rain.
    B. To see in the fog.
    C. To navigate construction areas.
    D. To signal other drivers to move.

Correct Answer is C. To navigate construction areas. Use low-beam headlights in the rain and fog.

175. You must stop before hitting the limit line when approaching a stop sign. This line is:

    A. Solid white and crosses your driving lane.
    B. Broken white and crosses your driving lane.
    C. Solid yellow and crosses your driving lane.
    D. Broken yellow and crosses your driving lane.

Correct Answer is A. Solid white and crosses your driving lane.

176. When you pass other cars on a three-lane highway, which lane should you use?

    A. The right lane
    B. The left lane
    C. The center lane
    D. The intersection

Correct Answer is B. The left lane. If three lanes of traffic are going in one direction, use the left-most lane to pass, drive faster, or turn left.

177. When should you NEVER pass another car?

    A. When the other car is driving too slow
    B. When the other car is driving too fast
    C. When there are broken yellow lines on the road
    D. When you enter an intersection

Correct Answer is D. When you enter an intersection. You may only pass on the roadway; never in an intersection.

178. When you feel that your tire pops or has gone flat, what should you do first?

    A. Veer left
    B. Veer right
    C. Keep straight
    D. Brake

Correct Answer is C. Keep straight. Don't speed up or slam the brakes. Keep the car straight until you can turn off somewhere. Hold the wheel tightly to keep the car under control.

179. When you see a triangular orange sign on the back of another vehicle, what does this mean?

    A. That vehicle must travel over 25 mph.
    B. That vehicle can only travel under 25 mph.
    C. That vehicle must travel over 35 mph.
    D. That vehicle can only travel under 35 mph.

Correct Answer is B. That vehicle can only travel under 25 mph. These signs can usually be seen on the backs of tractors and maintenance vehicles.

180. Which line on the road tells that you can pass on two-lane highways?

    A. Broken yellow line
    B. Solid yellow line
    C. Solid white line
    D. Broken white line

Correct Answer is A. Broken yellow line. Broken white lines indicate lanes you can pass when traffic moves in the same direction.

181. Flashing arrow signs indicate:

    A. Curves.
    B. Closures.
    C. Open roads.
    D. Slopes.

Correct Answer is B. Closures. These signs light up to indicate work zones at specific times of day and night or all the time.

182. Double solid yellow lines mean that passing on this road:

    A. Is always allowed.
    B. Is never allowed.
    C. Is allowed at certain times of day.
    D. Is allowed for certain kinds of vehicles.

Correct Answer is B. Is never allowed. These lines indicate traffic moving in opposite directions on a two-lane road. Passing is never allowed.

183. Traffic in roundabouts always travel:

    A. Straight.
    B. Clockwise.
    C. Counterclockwise.
    D. The direction indicated by the signs.

Correct Answer is C. Counterclockwise.

184. You should use your horn:

    A. To alert other drivers.
    B. To alert pedestrians.
    C. To alert blind people.
    D. To alert cyclists.

Correct Answer is A. To alert other drivers. Never honk your horn at pedestrians or cyclists.

185. When a driver signals with their hand and arm straight out, what does this mean?

    A. They're about to turn left.
    B. They're about to turn right.
    C. They're about to stop.
    D. They're about to let you pass.

Correct Answer is A. They're about to turn left.

186. Flag persons on highways:

    A. Report accidents to the police.
    B. Slow vehicles to a new speed limit sign.
    C. Direct traffic through bad weather.
    D. Direct traffic through work zones.

Correct Answer is D. Direct traffic through work zones.

187. What is it called when your tires begin to drive on the surface of the water rather than on cement when driving on wet roads?

- A. Tailgating
- B. Slipping
- C. Skidding
- D. Hydroplaning

Correct Answer is D. Hydroplaning. The barrier between your tires and the road will continue to make you lose control over your car.

188. When turning right onto a two-lane road, make sure you enter the road:

- A. On the center lane.
- B. On the left lane.
- C. On the right lane.
- D. On the nearest lane to you.

Correct Answer is C. On the right lane. Watch for pedestrians as you turn from the right-most lane to the other right-most lane.

189. When a driver signals with their palm flat and their arm and hand pointed down, they are about to:

    A. Turn right.
    B. Turn left.
    C. Speed up.
    D. Slow down.

Correct Answer is D. Slow down.

190. When making a right turn at an intersection, approach the turn:

    A. From the shoulder.
    B. From the center lane.
    C. From the right lane.
    D. From the left lane.

Correct Answer is C. From the right lane. Turn from the lane nearest to the lane you're turning into.

191. When on a one-way road, a solid yellow line is a:

    A. Left-edge line.
    B. Right-edge line.
    C. Centerline.
    D. No passing line.

Correct Answer is A. Left-edge line.

192. When entering a curve, you need to watch for oncoming cars. Make sure you:

    A. Speed up and turn on your headlights to signal.
    B. Honk your horn as you enter the curve.
    C. Slow down and move to the right side.
    D. Slow down and move to the left side.

Correct Answer is C. Slow down and move to the right side. This applies to curves as well as when you're driving up and over a hill.

193. On two-way roads with center lanes, cars can use the center lane to:

    A. Turn left and make U-turns.
    B. Turn right and make U-turns.
    C. Slow down and pass other cars.
    D. Speed up and pass other cars.

Correct Answer is A. Turn left and make U-turns.

194. With any turning vehicle, the rear wheels follow a_____ than the front wheels.

    A. Longer path
    B. Shorter path
    C. Slower path
    D. Same-sized path

Correct Answer is B. Shorter. This is why large trucks will often need to swing wide to the left in order to complete a right turn.

195. Right of way does NOT mean that you should:

    A. Give cars right of way even when police officers signal otherwise.
    B. Yield to pedestrians when you have the right of way.
    C. Yield to vehicles coming from the left at an unmarked intersection.
    D. Yield to vehicles coming from the right at an unmarked intersection.

Correct Answer is C. Yield to vehicles coming from the left at an unmarked intersection. Drivers from the left yield to you at an unmarked intersection with no signals or signs. You must yield to drivers on the right.

196. When signaling a right-hand turn with your arm, you must put your:

    A. Arm bent and hand extended up.
    B. Arm bent and hand extended down.
    C. Arm and hand extended out.
    D. Arm and hand extended to the right.

Correct Answer is A. Arm bent and hand extended up. Do not signal in the direction of your turn. Use the universal turn signal.

197. When approaching pedestrians using unmarked crosswalks, you should:

    A. Slow down and drive cautiously.
    B. Speed up to get over the crosswalk.
    C. Yield to the person in the road.
    D. Honk to alert the pedestrian.

Correct Answer is C. Yield to the person in the road. Whether crosswalks are marked or unmarked, drivers must yield to pedestrians.

198. Divided highways use _____ lines as the left edge of the road.

    A. Single solid yellow
    B. Single solid white
    C. Double solid yellow
    D. Double solid white

Correct Answer is A. Single solid yellow.

199. Which of these right of way rules is correct?

    A. Vehicles don't have to yield at crosswalks when they have the right of way.
    B. At unmarked T-intersections, cars on terminating roads must yield.
    C. Vehicles exiting a private driveway have the right of way.
    D. Right of way applies equally to people, bicycles, and cars.

Correct Answer is B. At unmarked T-intersections, cars on terminating roads must yield. Cars driving on the through-road have the right of way in this situation.

200. At near-freezing temperatures, road surfaces can become slippery. Which freezes first?

    A. Roads
    B. Bridges
    C. Slopes
    D. All at the same time

Correct Answer is B. Bridges. Since there's no ground beneath a bridge to hold in heat, they freeze faster than normal roads.

201. It is not legal to cross a solid double yellow line on your left when you want to:

    A. Pass.
    B. U-turn.
    C. Turn left.
    D. Enter a driveway.

Correct Answer is A. Pass. Cars may cross double solid yellow lines if they need to, but never to pass into traffic going in the opposite direction.

202. Why should cars never drive beside motorcycles in the same lane?

    A. Motorcycles can't signal.
    B. Motorcycles can't honk.
    C. Motorcycles need as much room as a car.
    D. Motorcycles can distract other drivers.

Correct Answer is C. Motorcycles need as much room as a car. Even in wide lanes, cars should never share a lane beside a motorcycle.

203. What do you call the connecting series of ramps between a freeway and another freeway or road?

    A. Acceleration lane
    B. Deceleration lane
    C. Exit ramp
    D. Interchange

Correct Answer is D. Interchange. This road helps drivers safely pass between freeways without obstructing traffic.

204. When driving slowly on a two-lane road, when must you pull over and let cars behind you pass?

    A. When there are 3 cars behind you
    B. When there are 4 cars behind you
    C. When there are 5 cars behind you
    D. When there are 6 cars behind you

Correct Answer is C. When there are 5 cars behind you. This number of cars unable to pass is considered unsafe.

205. When driving on two-lane roads, you can only pass cars on the left when there is a:

    A. Broken yellow line in your lane.
    B. Double solid yellow line in your lane.
    C. Broken double yellow line in your line.
    D. Solid white line in your lane.

Correct Answer is A. Broken yellow line in your lane.

206. Before re-entering traffic from a parallel park on the right-hand side of the road, you should always:

    A. Signal a left turn, look over your left shoulder.
    B. Signal a left turn, look over your right shoulder.
    C. Signal a right turn, look over your right shoulder.
    D. Signal a right turn, look over your left shoulder.

Correct Answer is A. Signal a left turn, look over your left shoulder.

207. When passing another vehicle:

    A. You should always slow down.
    B. You should still observe the speed limit.
    C. You can pass multiple cars if you can do so safely.
    D. You can follow another car making the same pass.

Correct Answer is B. You should still observe the speed limit. Some states unofficially permit the speed limit to be broken within a few mph as cars pass each other. However, in most cases, you must still observe the speed limit when passing.

208. When you approach a non-blinking yellow light at an intersection, what should you do?

    A. Stop immediately and watch for pedestrians.
    B. Stop immediately and wait for a red light.
    C. Slow down and drive with caution no matter what.
    D. Slow down and drive with caution, or stop safely.

Correct Answer is D. Slow down and drive with caution, or stop safely. When you see a steady yellow light, you know the red one is coming next. Proceed with caution or stop safely if you can.

209. When you see an unblinking yellow arrow at an intersection, what light will it turn into?

    A. Green light
    B. Red light
    C. Red arrow
    D. Any of the above

Correct Answer is D. Any of the above. A steady yellow arrow could turn into any of these, depending on its use. The correct action is to cautiously stop to see which one it is.

210. The outer edges of roads are marked by what kind of line?

    A. Broken white
    B. Solid white
    C. Broken yellow
    D. Solid yellow

Correct Answer is B. Solid white. These lines can only be crossed by cars moving to and from the shoulder of the road.

211. When school buses flash yellow lights, what should you do?

    A. Accelerate to pass them quickly.
    B. Stop quickly behind them.
    C. Slow down and get ready to stop.
    D. Slow down and safely pass.

Correct Answer is C. Slow down and get ready to stop. The bus will soon flash its red lights, so be prepared to stop, and don't pass.

212. When you see a sign with a curved arrow and the number 35, what does this mean?

    A. The curve ahead is 35 degrees.
    B. The maximum speed on the curve is 35 mph.
    C. The minimum speed on the curve is 35 mph.
    D. The recommended safe speed on the curve is 35 mph in normal conditions.

Correct Answer is D. The recommended safe speed on the curve is 35 mph in normal conditions.

213. When you arrive at an intersection at about the same time as another car without any lights or signs to tell you who has the right of way, what should you do?

    A. Yield if you're going straight.
    B. Yield if you're on the right.
    C. Yield if you're on the left.
    D. Yield just to be safe.

Correct Answer is C. Yield if you're on the left. It's not safe to yield for no reason because the other car won't know what you're doing.

214. What should you do at a stop sign?

    A. Come to a complete stop and then drive forward cautiously.
    B. Slow down and drive cautiously if the intersection is clear.
    C. Turn around to avoid a road closure.
    D. Stop and then yield to traffic.

Correct Answer is D. Stop and then yield to traffic. Only proceed once the road is clear.

215. A speed limit sign is a:

    A. Maximum speed limit.
    B. Minimum speed limit.
    C. Recommended speed limit.
    D. Daytime speed limit.

Correct Answer is A. Maximum speed limit. You cannot exceed the number printed on the sign in this area.

216. What does a yield sign mean?

    A. Slow down and watch for traffic without stopping.
    B. Slow down and prepare to stop for pedestrians.
    C. Keep a steady speed while other cars yield to your lane.
    D. Stop at the sign to give any pedestrians a chance to cross.

Correct Answer is B. Slow down and prepare to stop for pedestrians. Don't come to a stop unless you need to. Drive cautiously.

217. One thing you should make sure you do during your driving test is:

    A. Maintain a 2-second following distance.
    B. Use the left lane.
    C. Signal only when you see other cars in the way.
    D. Keep both hands on the wheel.

Correct Answer is D. Keep both hands on the wheel.

218. If you commit a traffic violation and a police officer stops you, what documents can they ask you to show?

    A. License, registration, social security card
    B. License, social security card, insurance information
    C. License, insurance information, working VISA
    D. License, registration, insurance information

Correct Answer is D. License, registration, insurance information.

219. If a vehicle is driving toward you in your lane, what should you do?

    A. Slam the brakes to avoid hitting them.
    B. Veer to the left as far as you can.
    C. Slow down and let them pass.
    D. Flash your lights, honk your horn, and veer right.

Correct Answer is D. Flash your lights, honk your horn, and veer right.

220. Who has the right of way when vehicles stop at a four-way stop?

    A. Whichever vehicle signals first
    B. Whichever vehicle was the last to stop
    C. Whichever vehicle was the first to stop
    D. Whichever vehicle is the largest

Correct Answer is C. Whichever vehicle was the first to stop.

221. When parking on a busy road, if you must, where should you park?

    A. Far from traffic
    B. Far from the curb
    C. Far from the yellow line
    D. Far from the walkway

Correct Answer is A. Far from traffic. Park as close to the curb as you can.

222. When approaching a school crosswalk, what is the speed limit?

    A. 10 mph
    B. 15 mph
    C. 20 mph
    D. 25 mph

Correct Answer is B. 15 mph.

223. When a school bus is stopped with its stop sign extended, you must:

    A. Slow down and drive cautiously.
    B. Stop if you are going the same direction as the bus.
    C. Stop if you are going in the opposite direction of the bus.
    D. Stop no matter which direction you're going.

Correct Answer is D. Stop no matter which direction you're going.

224. If you hear the siren of an emergency vehicle, you should:

    A. Look around to see if the vehicle is in your lane.
    B. Veer to the right and drive cautiously.
    C. Slow down and let the vehicle pass you.
    D. Stop on the right side of the road.

Correct Answer is D. Stop on the right side of the road. When you hear an emergency siren, the important thing is to get out of the way as quickly as possible.

225. Pedestrians that are illegally crossing a street without a crosswalk have the right of way.

    A. True
    B. False

Correct Answer is A. True. Pedestrians in the road always have the right of way.

226. If the roads are wet, you should:

    A. Use your low-beam headlights.
    B. Slow down.
    C. Speed up.
    D. Pump your brakes ever so often.

Correct Answer is B. Slow down. When roads are wet, increase the room you need to stop. The safe thing to do is reduce your speed.

227. When entering a roadway from a driveway, what should you do?

    A. Stop right before the sidewalk.
    B. Flash your headlights before entering the street.
    C. Honk your horn before entering the street.
    D. Back up gradually without stopping.

Correct Answer is A. Stop right before the sidewalk. You need to check to make sure the roads are clear.

228. Where should you look while backing up your car?

    A. Through the side mirrors
    B. Through the rear window
    C. Through the driving mirror
    D. Through the rear-view mirrors

Correct Answer is B. Through the rear window. Turn your body around to look out the rear window when backing up. Don't rely on mirrors, as they can distort the view around your car.

229. What is the maximum speed limit in a residential area when there is no posted sign?

    A. 45 mph
    B. 35 mph
    C. 25 mph
    D. 15 mph

Correct Answer is C. 25 mph.

230. What does a yellow line in the center of the road indicate?

    A. One-way traffic
    B. Two-way traffic
    C. A school zone
    D. A turn lane

Correct Answer is B. Two-way traffic. Traffic on either side of the line is moving in opposite directions. It is not legal to pass here.

231. For how long should you signal before turning?

    A. At least 2 seconds
    B. At least 4 seconds
    C. At least 6 seconds
    D. At least 8 seconds

Correct Answer is B. At least 4 seconds.

232. If a crosswalk is within _____ feet of your car, it is illegal to park there.

    A. 10 feet
    B. 15 feet
    C. 20 feet
    D. 25 feet

Correct Answer is C. 20 feet.

233. When a police officer flashes sirens and/or lights behind you, you should slam your brakes to stop in the road as quickly as possible.

    A. True
    B. False

Correct Answer is B. False. Drivers must show their cooperation by turning their signal on, yielding to the right side of the road, and pulling over, not slamming their brakes in the road.

234. Should you put your car in park when a police officer stops you?

    A. Yes
    B. No

Correct Answer is A. Yes.

235. Failing to remove snow from a vehicle can result in being fined.

    A. True
    B. False

Correct Answer is A. True.

236. If there's a firearm in the car when a police officer stops your car, you should:

    A. Brake immediately.
    B. Flash your signal.
    C. Keep your hands on the wheel.
    D. Take out the firearm to give it to the officer.

Correct Answer is C. Keep your hands on the wheel. Never take out a firearm without a police officer requesting it first.

237. Is accepting a police officer's citation an admission of guilt?

    A. Yes

    B. No

Correct Answer is B. No. The results of the citation depend on the results of your case. Accepting the citation is not an admission of guilt. Do as the officer tells you.

238. When a fender bender results in no or minor injuries, what should you do with your vehicle?

    A. Keep it on the road.

    B. Move it to the side of the road.

    C. Honk and turn on the emergency flashers.

    D. Both A and C

Correct Answer is B. Move it to the side of the road. If there are no injuries and the car is functional, move it safely to the side of the road until officers arrive.

239. To prevent hydroplaning, drive:

    A. Faster.
    B. On the lowest point of the road.
    C. On the highest point of the road.
    D. While coasting on the brakes.

Correct Answer is C. On the highest point of the road. Hydroplaning is less severe where there's less water on the road.

240. What is a deceleration lane?

    A. A lane where slow drivers can safely pass.
    B. A lane where fast drivers can safely pass.
    C. An extra lane at the exit of a highway.
    D. An exit lane at the entrance of an intersection.

Correct Answer is C. An extra lane at the exit of a highway. This gives cars the chance to slow down as they reduce their speed to match the new flow of traffic.

241. What does a vehicle tend to do at a curve?

    A. Decelerate
    B. Accelerate
    C. Go straight
    D. Go along the curve

Correct Answer is C. Go straight. Adjust your turn's compensation based on your speed, the road conditions, and the sharpness of the curve.

242. High-beam headlights are useful in which situation?

    A. Driving in open country without traffic.
    B. Driving in residential areas with no lights.
    C. Signaling to other drivers to warn of emergencies.
    D. Cutting through thick fog to see the road.

Correct Answer is A. Driving in open country without traffic. Headlights are not signals. High-beam headlights reflect off the fog and *reduce* visibility.

243. At a minimum, how many feet must you stay away from a fire hydrant when you park?

    A. 40 feet
    B. 30 feet
    C. 20 feet
    D. 10 feet

Correct Answer is D. 10 feet.

244. Illegally applying for a driver's license can result in imprisonment.

    A. True
    B. False

Correct Answer is A. True. Check with your state's DMV to make sure, but don't apply for a license illegally, no matter the consequences.

245. Where should child safety seats be installed?

    A. The front seat.
    B. The back seat.
    C. The passenger's lap.
    D. The trunk.

Correct Answer is B. The back seat. The front of the car takes the brunt of a collision. Children are safer in the rear seats.

246. What is the safest way to enter a curve?

    A. Speed up after entering.
    B. Speed up before entering.
    C. Slow down before entering.
    D. Slow down after entering.

Correct Answer is C. Slow down before entering.

247. How close can you legally park to a stop sign?

    A. 20 feet
    B. 30 feet
    C. 40 feet
    D. 50 feet

Correct Answer is B. 30 feet.

248. With no signals or signs at a place where two or more roads join together, you should always:

    A. Veer right to let oncoming traffic pass.
    B. Turn left to continue in your lane.
    C. Yield to traffic on the left because they have the right of way.
    D. Slow down and prepare to stop.

Correct Answer is D. Slow down and prepare to stop. No one has the right of way in this situation. You just need to be prepared to stop depending on what other drivers do. Reduce speed to better assess the situation.

249. If a railroad crossing is flashing its lights:

    A. Slow down and look up the tracks.
    B. Stop as close to the tracks as possible.
    C. Slow down and honk your horn as you cross.
    D. Stop 15 feet or more from the crossing.

Correct Answer is D. Stop 15 feet or more from the crossing.

250. Drivers who complete driver improvement programs are placed on probation for:

    A. 3 months
    B. 6 months
    C. 9 months
    D. 12 months

Correct Answer is D. 12 months.

251. If you drink just 5 ounces of wine, you've consumed as much alcohol as:

A. A 12 oz bottle of whiskey.
B. A 12 oz bottle of beer.
C. A 6 oz glass of vodka.
D. Two cans of beer.

Correct Answer is B. A 12 oz bottle of beer.

252. What should you do when you miss your exit on a highway?

A. Veer off the road and back up from the shoulder.
B. Slow down and back up, checking for cars first.
C. Make a U-turn back to your exit.
D. Go to the next exit.

Correct Answer is D. Go to the next exit. You can't turn around on a highway. Exit as soon as you can using the highway's exit ramps.

253. Unless a sign says otherwise, you can turn right at red lights after you:

    A. Check for traffic both ways.
    B. Make a full stop.
    C. Use your turn signal.
    D. All of the above

Correct Answer is D. All of the above.

254. Can you be fined for idling your car for 5 minutes on a road?

    A. Yes
    B. No

Correct Answer is A. Yes.

255. The vehicle you use for the driving test may not have:

    A. Inspection stickers.
    B. Out of state registrations.
    C. Obstructions between the driver and tester.
    D. All of the Above

Correct Answer is C. Obstructions between the driver and tester.

256. Over-the-counter medications can affect basic driving skills.

    A. True
    B. False

Correct Answer is A. True.

257. If you drive over private or public property to avoid a traffic sign or signal, you will receive:

    A. License suspension.

    B. Jail time.

    C. A 2-point moving violation.

    D. Both A and C

Correct Answer is C. A 2-point moving violation. You can also receive a fine.

258. What do diamond-shaped road signs indicate?

    A. Yield

    B. Stop

    C. Construction

    D. School

Correct Answer is C. Construction. Construction and warning signs are shaped like diamonds.

259. Having a fake driver's license could result in:

    A. A suspension and fine.
    B. A suspension only.
    C. A suspension, fine, and prison time.
    D. A court appearance.

Correct Answer is C. A suspension, fine, and prison time.

260. Who is required to wear a seat belt?

    A. The driver
    B. The driver and front-seat passengers
    C. The driver and back-seat passengers
    D. The driver and all passengers

Correct Answer is D. The driver and all passengers.

261. Aggressive drivers:

A. Refuse to yield even when other cars have the right of way.
B. Tailgate other cars.
C. Change lanes often.
D. All of the above

Correct Answer is D. All of the above. Any of these can indicate an aggressive driver.

262. The 3-second rule helps you know:

A. When to brake to get out of a skid
B. When yellow lights will turn red
C. How far to follow from another car
D. How fast to drive to match the speed limit

Correct Answer is C. How far to follow from another car.

263. With double yellow lines where one side is broken:

    A. You can pass from that side when safe.
    B. You can never pass from that side.
    C. Passing is never allowed.
    D. Passing is always allowed.

Correct Answer is A. You can pass from that side when safe.

264. What is the most common and difficult type of parking on a city street?

    A. Angle
    B. Parallel
    C. Downhill
    D. Uphill

Correct Answer is B. Parallel

265. You can cross the double solid yellow lines, so long as it's safe.

    A. True
    B. False

Correct Answer is B. False.

266. If you need to pass a bus, you should always:

    A. Honk first.
    B. Flash your signals.
    C. Increase following distance.
    D. Pass on the right side.

Correct Answer is C. Increase following distance. This is so the driver can see you in his rear-view mirror before you pass.

267. If driving in snow, turn on your:

    A. Wipers and defroster.
    B. Wipers and high-beam headlights.
    C. Wipers and low-beam headlights.
    D. Wipers and radio.

Correct Answer is C. Wipers and low-beam headlights

268. If your gas pedal starts to stick and you hear the motor speeding up:

    A. Turn off the car.
    B. Pump your brakes.
    C. Shift into neutral.
    D. Accelerate until it stops sticking.

Correct Answer is C. Shift into neutral. Keep your eyes on the road and pull off when it's safe to do so. Then, turn off the engine.

269. Moped drivers must be at least ___ years of age.

     A. 14
     B. 16
     C. 21
     D. 25

Correct Answer is B. 16.

270. How many seconds ahead should safe drivers focus their eyes?

     A. 0-10 seconds
     B. 10-20 seconds
     C. 20-30 seconds
     D. 30-40 seconds

Correct Answer is C. 20-30 seconds.

271. When another car is trying to pass you, what should you do?

    A. Slow down.
    B. Speed up.
    C. Move into the no-passing lane.
    D. Turn into the lane of the car passing you.

Correct Answer is A. Slow down. By maintaining a steady speed or slowing down, you can let the other driver safely pass you.

272. What do vertical regulatory signs tell you?

    A. Warnings about hazards
    B. Instructions about the law
    C. Information about upcoming turns
    D. The speed limit on the road ahead

Correct Answer is B. Instructions about the law. Other signs inform you about hazards, turns, and speed limits.

273. Cars driving on unmarked rural roads have a speed limit of:

    A. 25 mph.
    B. 35 mph.
    C. 45 mph.
    D. Whatever the driving conditions safely allow.

Correct Answer is B. 35 mph.

274. Hazardous driving conditions should make you increase your following distance from other cars by:

    A. 2x
    B. 3x
    C. 4x
    D. Nothing

Correct Answer is A. 2x. Double your following distance to stay safe on wet or hazardous roads.

275. If an approaching vehicle is at least ___ feet from your car, you should not use your high-beam headlights.

    A. 100 feet
    B. 300 feet
    C. 500 feet
    D. 1000 feet

Correct Answer is C. 500 feet.

276. Which of these things should you NOT use when driving through heavy rain?

    A. Windshield wipers
    B. High-beam headlights
    C. Reduced speed
    D. Turn signals

Correct Answer is B. High-beam headlights. High-beam headlights reflect off the rain and obstruct your view. Use your wipers, turn signals, and low-beam headlights while reducing your speed on wet roads.

277. Yellow painted curbs:

    A. Allow passenger cars to park to load or unload people.
    B. Allow people with disabilities to park.
    C. Allow anyone to park temporarily.
    D. Allow passenger cars to load or unload people without parking.

Correct Answer is D. Allow passenger cars to load or unload people without parking. The driver must stay with the car and only park long enough to let everyone out or in.

278. What kind of pedestrians are involved in crashes the most?

    A. Young
    B. Old
    C. Adults under the influence
    D. All of the above

Correct Answer is D. All of the above. These three types of people represent the most crashes involving pedestrians.

279. When you're driving slower than 35 mph, what should your following distance be?

    A. 1 second
    B. 2 seconds
    C. 3 seconds
    D. 4 seconds

Correct Answer is B. 2 seconds.

280. If someone sells a fake driver's license or ID, what is the charge?

    A. Larceny
    B. Felony
    C. Class 1 misdemeanor
    D. Class 2 misdemeanor

Correct Answer is C. Class 1 misdemeanor. Selling a driver's license or suggesting that a document can be used as one results in a Class 1 misdemeanor, though this can vary by state.

281. In order to obtain a license at the age of 19 or older, how long must you have a learner's permit before applying?

    A. 30 days
    B. 60 days
    C. 90 days
    D. 6 months

Correct Answer is B. 60 days.

282. Do bicycles have the same right of way as motor vehicles?

    A. No
    B. Yes
    C. Under certain weather conditions
    D. At certain times of night

Correct Answer is B. Yes. They have the same right of way as cars. They must obey the same traffic regulations.

283. Headlights become legally required when visibility in inclement weather is reduced to:

    A. 100 feet
    B. 300 feet
    C. 500 feet
    D. 700 feet

Correct Answer is C. 500 feet.

284. Blind spots are:

    A. Angles that vision-impaired people have trouble seeing in.
    B. Spots on the road where visibility is reduced.
    C. Dangerous areas in mirrors that cannot easily be seen.
    D. Both B and C

Correct Answer is C. Dangerous areas in mirrors that cannot easily be seen. Areas that are hard to see on the side of your car through your mirrors are considered your blind spots.

285. What is the color of signs that warn you of hazardous road conditions?

    A. Red
    B. Black
    C. Yellow
    D. White

Correct Answer is C. Yellow. Unexpected roadway conditions and hazards are displayed on yellow signs.

286. If a broken yellow line is on your side of the road, but a solid yellow line is on the opposite side, can you pass cars?

    A. No, because the lanes are traveling in opposite directions.
    B. No, because you can never cross yellow lines.
    C. Yes, because you can cross broken yellow lines if it is safe.
    D. Yes, because you can always cross yellow lines.

Correct Answer is C. Yes, because you can cross broken yellow lines if it is safe.

287. How should you keep children under 4 years old safe in the car?

    A. With a booster seat
    B. With a safety belt
    C. With an airbag
    D. With a rear-facing safety seat

Correct Answer is D. With a rear-facing safety seat. Children under 4 should not be near airbags, restrained only by a seatbelt or in booster seats.

288. Motorcyclists have the right to use the full width of the lane:

    A. So long as the speed limit is lower than 35 mph.
    B. So long as the speed limit is higher than 35 mph.
    C. On multi-lane roads.
    D. On every road.

Correct Answer is D. On every road. Cars must pass motorcyclists as though they are other cars. Don't share a lane with a motorcycle—give them the full width of the lane.

289. You can drive faster than the maximum speed limit:

    A. Never.
    B. To keep up with traffic.
    C. When weather conditions allow it.
    D. When driving in the left or fast lane.

Correct Answer is A. Never. The maximum speed limit should be observed no matter what other drivers are doing.

290. In order to see while driving at night, make sure you:

    A. Turn on the light inside your car.
    B. Don't overdrive your headlights.
    C. Stay focused on the road's right-hand side.
    D. Stay focused on the road's left-hand side.

Correct Answer is B. Don't overdrive your headlights. When visibility is low, make sure you don't drive faster than the space you can see in your headlights.

291. If you leave the scene of a crash that results in at least $50 of damage, how many points will you get on your license?

    A. 2
    B. 4
    C. 6
    D. 8

Correct Answer is C. 6.

292. When driving in heavy traffic at night, use your _____ to see ahead of you.

    A. High-beam headlights
    B. Low-beam headlights
    C. Four-way flashers
    D. Parking lights

Correct Answer is B. Low-beam headlights. Never use your high-beams in heavy traffic, as it can blind other drivers.

293. When are you allowed to NOT stop for a school bus?

    A. When its red lights are flashing.
    B. When it's on the other side of a divided highway.
    C. When you have room to pass.
    D. You must always stop for a school bus.

Correct Answer is B. When it's on the other side of a divided highway. This is the only time you don't have to stop for a school bus.

294. Traffic lanes separated by a dotted white line:

    A. Can never be passed.
    B. Can always be passed when safe.
    C. Can only be passed at intersections.
    D. Can only be passed when signs indicate it's safe.

Correct Answer is B. Can always be passed when safe. Dotted white lines separate traffic moving in the same direction and can be passed if the road is clear.

295. When an intersection has no white stop line, where should you stop?

    A. Before the crosswalk.
    B. The stop sign.
    C. In the crosswalk, so long as no pedestrians are crossing.
    D. You should continue through the intersection.

Correct Answer is A. Before the crosswalk. Make sure pedestrians have room to walk, and proceed carefully through the intersection when it is safe to do so.

296. Alcohol is:

    A. A stimulant.
    B. A depressant.
    C. An analgesic.
    D. A methamphetamine.

Correct Answer is B. A depressant. This means that it disrupts the thoughts and neurochemical reactions that transmit signals between nerves.

297. What does a green arrow at an intersection mean?

    A. You can drive in that direction but must yield to other traffic.

    B. You can drive in that direction, but other traffic must yield to you.

    C. You can drive in that direction after stopping and making sure the road is clear.

    D. You can drive in that direction under certain conditions or times of day.

Correct Answer is A. You can drive in that direction but must yield to other traffic. So long as a green arrow is lit in your lane, oncoming lanes have a red light and must stop. You must still yield to traffic in the intersection as well as bicycles or pedestrians crossing the street.

298. If your car is skidding, you should:

    A. Slam the brakes.

    B. Slam the accelerator.

    C. Steer left if your rear is skidding left.

    D. Steer right if your rear is skidding left.

Correct Answer is C. Steer left if your rear is skidding left. Don't change your speed in a skid as this can make it worse.

299. When lanes are separated by dashed yellow lines, this means that you can:

    A. Never pass.
    B. Pass all the time.
    C. Pass so long as there's no oncoming traffic.
    D. Pass so long as you're on the left side of the road.

Correct Answer is C. Pass so long as there's no oncoming traffic. Dashed yellow lines indicate traffic moving in opposite directions that can pass using the other lane when it's safe to do so.

300. Do drivers making U-turns have to yield to other cars first?

    A. Yes, except for bicycles.
    B. Yes, including bicycles.
    C. No, they have the right of way.
    D. No, unless they're at a light.

Correct Answer is B. Yes, including bicycles. Drivers making U-turns must first yield to all other vehicles and bicycles.

301. Both sides of the road can cross double solid yellow lines so long as it's safe.

    A. True
    B. False

Correct Answer is B. False. No one can cross solid double yellow lines, which indicate traffic moving in opposite directions on roads that cannot be passed safely.

302. At what speed are you likely to start hydroplaning in heavy rain?

    A. 20 mph
    B. 30 mph
    C. 40 mph
    D. 50 mph

Correct Answer is D. 50 mph.

303. Which of these attributes does NOT affect the distance it takes for a car to successfully brake?

    A. The car's height.
    B. The car's speed.
    C. The road conditions.
    D. The tire conditions.

Correct Answer is A. The car's height.

304. When you are coming up to a road work zone, what should you do?

    A. Reduce your following distance.
    B. Increase your following distance.
    C. Watch the workers closely so you don't hit them.
    D. Turn on your hazard lights so everyone can see you.

Correct Answer is B. Increase your following distance. In construction zones, slow down, prepare to stop if necessary, and decrease your distance from other cars. Don't focus on the workers, and don't speed up.

305. When you see an emergency vehicle with its lights and sirens on, you must pull over to the side of the road unless:

    A. They have room to safely pass you.
    B. They aren't in your lane.
    C. They're on the other side of a divided highway.
    D. They look like they're about to turn around.

Correct Answer is C. They're on the other side of a divided highway. If the emergency vehicle is traveling in the same direction as you, you should always safely pull over to the side of the road to let them pass.

306. How far ahead can a bicycle rider see when riding at night using their white headlight?

    A. 100 feet.
    B. 250 feet.
    C. 500 feet.
    D. 1000 feet.

Correct Answer is C. Bicycles are required to have white lights that make the roads visible for 500 feet. Keep this distance in mind when watching for riders at night.

307. Speed limit signs show you how fast you can legally drive under all road conditions.

    A. True
    B. False

Correct Answer is B. False. Speed limit signs show you how fast you can legally drive under normal or ideal road conditions. Weather, construction, and other hazards reduce the maximum speed limit.

308. If your tire blows out, what should you do?

    A. Pull your car off the road when you can.
    B. Brake your car slowly.
    C. Steer straight without veering.
    D. All of the above

Correct Answer is D. All of the above. If your tire blows out, do not slam on your brakes. Try to retain control of your car by braking, and slowly pull off the side of the road.

309. When should your vehicle's lights be turned on?

    A. Always
    B. From 30 minutes before sunset to 30 minutes after sunrise
    C. From an hour before sunset to an hour after sunrise
    D. Never

Correct Answer is B. From 30 minutes before sunset to 30 minutes after sunrise. The lights on many vehicles still must be turned on manually to achieve this. Drivers during this timeframe must always use their lights.

310. When drivers approach an intersection to turn left at a turn signal, you can expect that they:

    A. Will stop in the intersection to check for cars.
    B. Will turn without stopping.
    C. Will not yield to oncoming traffic.
    D. Will not yield to pedestrians.

Correct Answer is B. Will turn without stopping. Drivers who make left-hand turns must yield to oncoming traffic and pedestrians, just as they must with right turns. However, if they have a left-hand turn signal, they are not required to stop before turning.

311. Many cyclists drive with headlights on their helmets at night. What is the visibility distance for these lights?

    A. 150 feet
    B. 300 feet
    C. 500 feet
    D. 650 feet

Correct Answer is C. 500 feet. These lights are built to be spotted by drivers from at least this far away to protect the cyclist on dark roads.

312. Does the size of your car affect the 10-second rule for safe passing space?

    A. Yes
    B. No

Correct Answer is A. Yes. While the 10-second rule suggests that you need this much distance between you and another car to pass safely, the size of your car is a major factor that can increase this required time.

313. What should you do at a flashing yellow light?

    A. Stop completely
    B. Merge with traffic
    C. Proceed cautiously
    D. Stop and watch for pedestrians

Correct Answer is C. Proceed cautiously. Flashing yellow lights do not require drivers to stop.

314. When you drink a 12 oz. beer, how long does it take for your body to flush out the alcohol on average?

    A. 5 hours
    B. 1 hour
    C. 30 minutes
    D. 10 minutes

Correct Answer is B. 1 hour. While a person's weight and other factors can affect this time, 1 hour is the average for when it's safe to drive after having just one beer.

315. For how long should a driver use their turn signal before turning onto an exit ramp?

    A. Right as they're making the turn
    B. 200 feet before the ramp
    C. 100 feet before the ramp
    D. 50 feet before the ramp

Correct Answer is C. 100 feet before the ramp.

316. When driving on an expressway:

    A. Trucks must reduce their speed.
    B. Drivers must think faster.
    C. The speed limit can be exceeded.
    D. Tailgating is less dangerous.

Correct Answer is B. Drivers must think faster. Car handling on an expressway is even more important than on regular streets. Drivers must think faster at higher speeds to stay safe.

317. After exiting an expressway, make sure you:

    A. Double your following distance.
    B. Check your speedometer and slow down.
    C. Check your tire pressure.
    D. Maintain the same speed.

Correct Answer is B. Check your speedometer and slow down. Ordinary roads have reduced speed limits compared to expressways. Make sure you check your speed after exiting the ramp to adjust to the new speed limit.

318. If you have a poor driving record, you may be facing:

    A. Increased police surveillance.
    B. Increased registration renewal fees.
    C. Increased insurance rates.
    D. Increased risk for accidents.

Correct Answer is C. Increased insurance rates. Poor driving records do not affect the cost of renewing your license. However, auto insurance companies can hike your rates after deciding that you are more of a risk based on your records.

319. When a truck is starting to pass you on the road, make sure you:

    A. Keep to the left side of your lane.
    B. Keep to the right side of your lane.
    C. Honk lightly to make sure he sees you.
    D. Stop to make sure he can pass.

Correct Answer is B. Keep to the right side of your lane. Trucks may need extra room to pass, so try to drive further from the center of the road while they do so.

320. Look farther ahead when driving on a freeway compared to city and residential districts because:

    A. Traffic will be further ahead of you.
    B. There aren't many signs to see.
    C. Road hazards are harder to spot.
    D. Traffic will be closer to you.

Correct Answer is C. Road hazards are harder to spot. This is due to increased speeds. Look farther ahead to give yourself more time to stop.

321. What is NOT required for your driving test?

    A. Vehicle registration card
    B. Vehicle window registration sticker
    C. Valid auto insurance card
    D. That you own the car

Correct Answer is D. That you own the car. The DMV always checks your registration and insurance as well as your car's functionality, including wipers, lights, signals, and mirrors. However, you can use a car you do not own, such as your parents', for the driving test.

322. What is the main mistake new drivers make when trying to do a three-point turn?

    A. Not turning the wheel far enough
    B. Turning the wheel too far
    C. Backing up too fast
    D. Taking too much time

Correct Answer is A. Not turning the wheel far enough. Novice drivers often make turns with 4 or 5 "points" because they don't turn the wheel far enough, especially in the first maneuver.

323. What is a rolling stop?

    A. Trying to stop on a hill
    B. An incomplete stop
    C. Trying to stop on bad brakes
    D. Try to pull off while going too fast

Correct Answer is B. An incomplete stop. Especially at stop signs, rolling stops can be dangerous. Drivers who do not come to a full and complete stop reduce their ability to see the oncoming lanes before turning.

324. Never turn your head when changing lanes.

    A. True
    B. False

Correct Answer is B. False. In addition to signaling and checking your mirrors, you should turn your head to look for cars and cyclists in your blind spot before changing lanes.

325. When merging with traffic on a freeway, make sure you:

    A. Come close to stopping at the end of the ramp.
    B. Completely stop at the end of the ramp.
    C. Adjust your speed to merge with traffic without stopping.
    D. Wait in the acceleration lane first.

Correct Answer is C. Adjust your speed to merge with traffic without stopping. While you should always stop if it's unsafe to merge, as a rule, you should not stop in the acceleration lane or in the entrance ramp. Signal so other drivers know you're turning, and adjust your speed to safely merge.

Made in the USA
Las Vegas, NV
28 April 2022